Rochester & Olmsted County
Celebrating 150 Years
An Historic Photo Album

Acknowledgments

This book celebrates the sesquicentennial of Rochester and Olmsted County and is dedicated to the pioneers who shared this river basin with a small band of Dakota Indians and those who followed.

Our thanks to the Olmsted County History Center for the use of images from its extensive collection of historic photographs and helping put together the links of this historic chain.

We also thank the Post-Bulletin and its library assistants for research and photographs, especially of the later years of the history.

This book relied upon the several histories written about Rochester and Olmsted County for factual details and a workable chronology, without which this project would not have been possible.

And last, but not least, we thank the volunteers putting together events for celebration of the 150th anniversary of the city and county for their enthusiastic support and encouragement.

This book has been made possible by the

Post-Bulletin

Olmsted County Historical Society

Since 1926, the Olmsted County Historical Society (OCHS) has collected, preserved and interpreted the history of Olmsted County, Minnesota by creating and maintaining a varied presentation of educational programs, special historical events and exhibits.

In addition to maintaining a Library and an historical museum at the Olmsted County History Center, the Society owns and operates five historic buildings and sites including Mayowood, the former home of three generations of the Mayo family.

The OCHS Library/Archives contains a vast collection of photographs, documents and other county memorabilia. Photographs in this book are representative of the material in the collection. Reproductions of photographs are available for purchase from the Olmsted County History Center.

A qualified staff manages the programs assisted by many enthusiastic volunteers. Visit us at 1195 West Circle Drive SW (County Road 22), Rochester, Minnesota. For more information call 507-282-9447 or visit our web site at www.olmstedhistory.com.

Copyright© 2003   •   ISBN: 1-932129-47-2

All rights reserved. No part of this book may be reproduced, stored in a retrieval system or transmitted in any form or by any means, electronic, mechanical, photocopying, recording or otherwise, without prior written permission of the copyright owner or the publisher.
Published by Pediment Publishing, a division of The Pediment Group, Inc. www.pediment.com   Printed in Canada

CELEBRATING 150 YEARS

TABLE OF CONTENTS

FOREWORD 4

THE FOUNDING 1853 - 1882 5

RUIN & REBIRTH 1883 - 1899 14

A NEW CENTURY 1900 - 1914 41

THE WAR YEARS 1915 - 1945 69

PEACE & PROSPERITY 1946 - 1977 100

FLOOD & REDEVELOPMENT 1978 - 1999 111

A NEW MILLENNIUM 2000 - TODAY 123

Foreword

In 1854, George Head hauled a log behind his oxen to create the first "street" in the city he named after Rochester, New York.

Head lived to see his fledgling settlement grow and prosper, eventually becoming the county seat of Olmsted County and the dominant population center of the county for the next 150 years.

Olmsted County was peopled by settlers seeking a new life in the opening western frontier. Its history is inevitably entwined with its rivers, prairie and woodlands and its location as a transportation hub. Events of history served to direct that it would become a hospitality and major medical center.

This book provides a glimpse into the history of Rochester and how it grew into a world-renowned medical center and one of Minnesota's major cities. The photos trace its founding and its near destruction in its early years to today.

Fascinating photographs relive the day-to-day lives of those who built the landmarks and institutions and guided the dynamic growth of Rochester, suffered when war, hardships and disaster struck and enjoyed ordinary workaday lives across the decades. Rochester's largest industry, health care, is followed from its humble beginnings to its economic leadership role in the 21st century.

Visit photographs of what we bought and sold and how we got around. Explore what has happened in arts and entertainment, education, the impact of diversity and technology and changing mores.

This book celebrates the sesquicentennial of Rochester and is dedicated to the pioneers who settled the city and those who followed, each making a contribution over the past 150 years.

The Founding 1853 - 1882

In 1853, Smith and Company built a cabin somewhere in what is now downtown Rochester and staked a claim. But the acknowledged founder of Rochester, George Head, jumped the Smith claim in July 1854. He subsequently paid $3,600 to settle the dispute and get title to the land.

The land was frontier rough, but rich, deep prairie soil and trees for lumber drew farmers and lumbermen to Head's claim, which he named after Rochester, New York. Easterners and those who landed in eastern seaports from across the Atlantic made their way into this area.

Between 1850 and 1857 the population of the Minnesota Territory soared from 6,077 to 150,000 and the Rochester region received its share of settlers.

As an indication of the importance of farming to the area's economy, by 1870 the population of Olmsted County was nearly 20,000, a quarter listed as foreign born. Rochester's urban population was only about 4,000.

Rochester's location on the Dubuque Trail, the stagecoach and wagon road from St. Paul to Dubuque, Iowa, made it a natural dropping-off point for many. The city's modern hospitality industry had an early start caring for travelers along the Dubuque Trail.

The second building in the city was a shanty built by Head as a hotel called Head's Tavern and then sold to Asa LeSueur in 1856. Broadway House, Cook House and the Bradley House were also early hotels serving the city.

While Olmsted County does not share in Minnesota's wealth of 10,000 lakes, it does have rivers and creeks. Mills took advantage of the swift-flowing Zumbro River to power grindstones, converting wheat into flour. The Chicago Northwestern Railroad came to Rochester in the late 1870 serving the city as did stage coaches which supplied transport in the 1860s.

All the trappings of a growing city sprang up in the early years with a growing number of churches, schools and even a Masonic temple. The Second State Hospital for the Insane opened on January 1, 1879, with a total of 50 patients by January 17 of that year, some transferred from St. Peter State Hospital.

Early agriculture in Oronoco Township, circa 1855. *Courtesy Olmsted County Historical Society*

THE FOUNDING 1853-1882

The Potsdam flour mills, built in 1861 by J.C. Baeton, R.O. Corinsky, E.A. Mielke and other pioneers of the town. The large windmill jutting from the roof was the source of power for the milling since there was no water power available in the area. The wind-powered mill served the farmers of Farmington Township for 15 years, but the lack of railroad facilities limited the towns' original aim of becoming a great flour manufacturing center. *Courtesy Olmsted County Historical Society*

Rochester street scene, 1864. *Courtesy Olmsted County Historical Society*

Rochester in 1868. From left around picture: Hamlet Easton dwelling, Huney's cabinet store, old barn, Issac Simond's home, Universalist Church, Central School, Episcopal Church, Courthouse, Congregational Church, Presbyterian Church, red brick library, vacant lot which later became the site of the Masonic Temple. *Courtesy Olmsted County Historical Society*

Rochester street scene, 1868. From 1860 to 1870, the population of Rochester grew from 1,424 to 3,953. Olmsted County had 15,364 naturalized citizens and 4,429 foreign born citizens, according to the census of 1870. *Courtesy Rochester Post-Bulletin*

THE FOUNDING 1853-1882

Lithograph of early Rochester, 1868, looking southwest. The population at that time was approximately 3,000. Included from left to right: Bradley House, Moe & Olds Mill, Gus Hargesheimer Drugs, Heaney Block, Congregational Church, Presbyterian Church, school, and the Courthouse. On the far right are the C&NW

Railway Station and Andusens Mill. In the right foreground in front of the covered bridge is the Oakwood Cemetery. *Courtesy Olmsted County Historical Society*

Lithograph of Broadway House, built in 1858 at 301 North Broadway by Charles H. Lindsley. It was leased by Olmsted County as the courthouse from 1858 to 1867. Nick Peters purchased the building in 1867 and operated it as a hotel known as the Broadway House. *Courtesy Olmsted County Historical Society*

Lithograph of early Eyota, from the Illustrated Historical Atlas of the State of Minnesota, 1874. *Courtesy Olmsted County Historical Society*

E.D. Buck's store, High Forest Township, 1870. Buck returned to High Forest in 1867 following Civil War service to engage in the mercantile business. Pictured, left to right: Charles Armstrong, Harry Johnson, Vet Johnson, E.D. Buck, and V. Dickey. *Courtesy Olmsted County Historical Society*

Robertson Brothers Implements located on Zumbro Street east of Broadway, 1873. Isaac Robertson is on the left; William Robertson on the right. The site was near the Great Western tracks on the north side of 2nd Street S. E. *Courtesy Olmsted County Historical Society*

THE FOUNDING 1853-1882

District #9 Pinewood School, 1878. The boys on the left are Bob Finch and Teddy Smith. Also included in the group seated are: Geneveve Kennedy, Addie Kennedy, Fred Finch, and Blanch Terry. The girl standing on the right is Delia Wood. *Courtesy Olmsted County Historical Society*

State Hospital Administration Building was built in 1877 and opened in 1879. It was replaced by a new building in 1952. *Courtesy Olmsted County Historical Society*

Group of High Forest ladies in front of the Masonic Hall, circa 1874. Back row, left to right: Mrs. N.E. Gaskill, Mrs. Fitzpatrick, Mrs. Waller, and Mrs. W.K. Tattersall. Middle row: Mrs. Z.K. Russell, Mrs. J.L. Rockwell, Mrs. Cyrus Converse, Miss Darcus Burton, Mrs. P.A. Honeywell, Mrs. E.D. Buck, and Mrs. Chet Lyon. Included in front row: Miss Wilcox, Mrs. Nathaniel Lyon, and Mrs. McCoy. *Courtesy Olmsted County Historical Society*

Campus of Rochester State Hospital, circa 1880. The first patients were admitted by transfer from St. Peter, January 1, 1879. *Courtesy Olmsted County Historical Society*

The "Grange Store" on Zumbro Street, circa 1876. John Robertson was the owner. *Courtesy Olmsted County Historical Society*

Oronoco, looking west from the location of the old school, 1879. The steel bridge was built in early 1879 and the mill burned later that year. *Courtesy Olmsted County Historical Society*

Cook House was built in 1869 at the corner of Broadway and 2nd Street S. W. The top two stories burned in February, 1947. First National Bank was in the hotel building from 1869 until 1949. *Courtesy Olmsted County Historical Society*

Ruin & Rebirth 1883 - 1899

A tornado blew through Kalmar Township, northwest of Byron, on July 21, 1883. That devastating twister, the *Rochester Post* newspaper reported, killed four and injured 20.

That tornado was the opening act for a storm exactly one month later in Rochester that killed 31 and injured more than 100. The twister devastated one-third of the prairie city and leaders called for aid from the state and in nearby states. More than $60,000 in relief funds were donated to the reconstruction effort.

The August 21, 1883, tornado proved to be a fateful wind, prompting the construction of Saint Marys Hospital and directing a small medical practice on its path to greatness.

The storm-shattered buildings and uprooted nature didn't stop progress. Dr. William Worral Mayo proposed a central water system and an electric plant for the city in 1886 to provide street lighting that had been provided by a local coal gas works called the Rochester Light & Fuel Co. The generating plant began producing electricity on March 15, 1894. The city built a sheriff's office and jail in 1888 and established a five-man police force. As the turn of the century approached, Broadway had become a wide thoroughfare lined with wooden storefronts with hitching posts stationed along both sides of the street. A city hall was built in 1884 at Third Street and First Avenue Southwest, where the public library was located.

The city's rail service began when a Winona & St. Peter Railroad train puffed into Rochester in summer of 1864. Adding to service was the Winona & Southwestern Railroad, with tracks running from Winona through High Forest Township. Grain elevators shipped to Midwestern markets and the passenger trains, linked to stagecoach routes, made the city a westward way station. It also brought patients for medical treatment, which in turn, brought demand for patient care, lodging and visitor services.

Northwest Rochester after the cyclone of 1883 caused extensive damage. The cyclone claimed 31 victims, injured more than 100 people and caused more than $100,000 in damage. *Courtesy Olmsted County Historical Society*

CELEBRATING 150 YEARS

Rochester street scene before the cyclone of 1883 struck. *Courtesy Olmsted County Historical Society*

The same scene following the destruction on August 21, 1883. *Courtesy Olmsted County Historical Society*

Cole's mill after the cyclone. The stove in the foreground was from the home of Paul Thompson, 8th Street N.E., which was leveled to the ground. *Courtesy Olmsted County Historical Society*

Van Dusen elevator near Chicago and Northwestern Railroad after the cyclone of August 1883. *Courtesy Olmsted County Historical Society*

T.P. Hall Buggy Works following the cyclone, 1883. Following the storm, relief totalling $75,293 came from all parts of the country. *Courtesy Olmsted County Historical Society*

South Broadway following the cyclone of August 21, 1883. The tin in the foreground is from the roof the Heaney Block where Dr. William W. Mayo set up a temporary hospital on the third floor to care for those injured in the cyclone. *Courtesy Olmsted County Historical Society*

View on Broadway following the cyclone of 1883. Every part of Rochester sustained some damage, though the worst damage was in the north part of town. *Courtesy Olmsted County Historical Society*

The first ambulance of the Mayo Clinic was custom made in 1875 for Father Rask of Saint Bridget's Church. *Courtesy Olmsted County Historical Society*

Marion School, December 15, 1885. James Chapman was the teacher. Fifth row, left to right: Charles Fawcett, Aurelia McCaleb, visitor, unknown, James Chapman, Myrtie Phelps, Kittie Skeels, Kate McCaleb, Lizzie Willie, and Jennie Porter. Fourth row: Arthur Fawcett, Earl Beach, Mary Cram, Mary Phelps, Luella McCaleb, Lib Kinney, Rose Campion, Fanny Bailey, Minnie Nickum, Myrtie Fawcett and May Van Camp. Third row: Bert Van Camp, Mayme Skeels, Matt Vail, Nora Watts, Ada Vail, Lill Strangeway, Jessie Emerson, Grace Strangeway, Joe Campbell and Will Campbell. Second row: Agnes Kinney, Ona Beach, Harry Campbell, Arthur Emerson, George Skeels, Nellie Campion, Jessie Mercer and Clara Haney. Front row: Jennie Berkins, Cora McCaleb, Walter Haney, Peter Beach, Will Chase, Violet Phelps, Clara Smith and Clar Mercer. *Courtesy Olmsted County Historical Society*

Rochester Seminary, 1886. Standing, left to right: Henry Williams, Minnie Gibbons, Jessie Varmyhlia, Mary Gammel, Nellie Lathrup, Myra Crowfoot, Elliotson Rogers, Will Vale, Sam Vermyhlia, Waitie Butterfield, Minnie Anderson and Ida Converse. Seated: Ida Haney, Ida Fizzell, Hattie Clough, Margaret Graham, Lizzie Lane, Carrie Dale, Enock Leonard, Edith Graham, Paul Goode and May Vale. *Courtesy Olmsted County Historical Society*

Picnic at Fugel's Mill, July 7, 1887. Back row, standing left to right: John M. Rowley, Mary Peck, Leslie Stillwell, Ruth Chadbourne, Sam Furlow, Spencer Knapp, Anna Cross (back of fan), Burt W. Eaton, Lucy DuBois and Clara F. Olds. Middle row: M.G. Denton, Inez Kinsbury, John J. Fulkerson, Hattie Smith and Miss Sayles. Front row: Miss Evans, Miss Gramling, Will Smith, Matie Knapp, Frank E. Gooding and Miss Evans. *Courtesy Olmsted County Historical Society*

Marion Band participating in a band tournament in Rochester, 1887. Band members included: band leader Louis E. Bragg, Len Kinney, Earl Beach, Bill Keane, Will Nickum, Herman Bach, Ed Bach, Howard Lull and George Newell. The picture was taken in front of the Cook Hotel. *Courtesy Olmsted County Historical Society*

Gathering in 1888 in front of the Bonner home in Stewartville. Back row, left to right: Mrs. John Owens, Edith Staples, Mrs. W.E. Smith, Mrs. Charles Stewart, Mrs. Lucinda Hutchins. Middle: Miss Mae Rolph, Mrs. Truman Horton, Mrs. D. Bonner, unknown, Mrs. Jim Kelly, Mrs. Heath, Mrs. Wilkins, Mrs. Hiram Sage, Mrs. William Tubbs, Mrs. Noah Staples, unknown, Mrs. Howard, Anna Tubbs and Mrs. John Brin, Sr. Front row: Mrs. George Ware and baby, Miss Howard, Miss Mattie Howard, Mrs. George Wilkins, Margaret Bonner (child), Mrs. Andrew Bonner, Mrs. George Tichnor, George Tichnor (boy) and Effie Tichnor (girl). *Courtesy Olmsted County Historical Society*

RUIN & REBIRTH 1883-1899

M.L. Dibble Blacksmithing at 112 W. 4th Street, 1889. His bicycle shop was to the left. In 1905, M. L. Dibble, pictured in the doorway, built the West hotel on these two sites. He later sold the hotel to the Kahler Corporation which built on a dining area; in 1957 this became the cafeteria "The Scandia." *Courtesy Olmsted County Historical Society*

New York Bazar, Mrs. W.S. Elkins's store, at 13 W. Zumbro in September 1890. *Courtesy Olmsted County Historical Society*

Chicago Northwestern Depot and yards, 1890. The first passenger train arrived in Rochester on October 12, 1864, on the Winona and St. Peter Railroad. It took more than three hours for the train to make the trip from Winona to Rochester. *Courtesy Olmsted County Historical Society*

Merchants Block, S. Broadway, circa 1891. *Courtesy Olmsted County Historical Society*

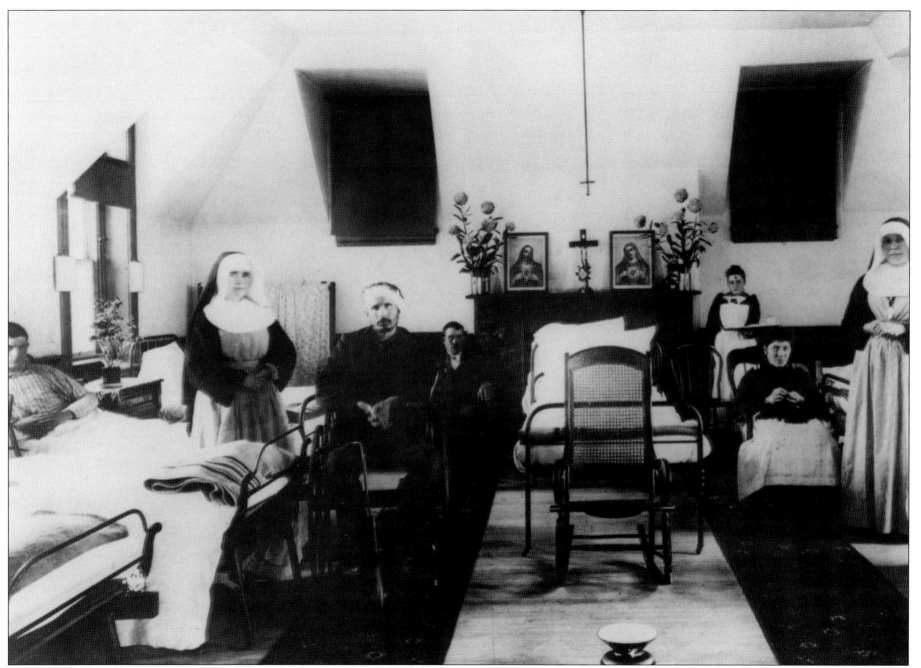
An early ward at St. Marys Hospital. The 27-bed hospital was established by the Sisters of St. Francis in 1889. The cyclone of 1883 is popularly credited as being responsible for the origin of both St. Marys Hospital and the Mayo Clinic. *Courtesy Olmsted County Historical Society*

William Worrall Mayo, center, and his sons Charles Horace, left, and William J., right, circa 1895. William J. graduated from Ann Arbor Medical School in 1883 and Charles graduated in 1888 from the Northwestern Medical School in Chicago.

W.W. Mayo was born in England in 1819 and came to this country as a young man. After becoming a physician, he practiced in a several communities before settling permanently in Rochester in the mid-1860s. He built a home on the corner of 2nd Avenue and 1st Street S.E. in 1863, the future site of the 1914 building of the Mayo Clinic. In January 1864, he brought his family from Le Seuer to live in their new Rochester home. At first a typical frontier doctor, he became more and more interested and skilled in the then-new field of surgery.

It was in large part thanks to his encouragement, example, and early teaching that his sons chose medicine as a career. Dr. William J. Mayo joined his father in practice in 1883. Dr. Charles Mayo became associated with his father and older brother in 1888.

Dr. W.W. Mayo practiced as a country doctor. *Courtesy Olmsted County Historical Society*

Rochester Public Library was located in the northwest room of the second floor of the old City Hall building, circa 1890. Miss Edna Emerick was the Librarian. *Courtesy Olmsted County Historical Society*

District #121 Lovelace School, Elmira Township, 1890. Mary E. McAdams was the teacher. *Courtesy Olmsted County Historical Society*

Hendricks & Olson grocery store, circa 1890. *Courtesy Olmsted County Historical Society*

Marion Brass Band, 1891. Back row, left to right: George Skeels, Lou Bragg, Frank Lowrie, Will Skells, Charles Bragg and Earl Beach. Front row: Jim Haney, Herman Bach, Jake Haney, Len Kenny and Charles Bolwine. *Courtesy Olmsted County Historical Society*

RUIN & REBIRTH 1883-1899

Pierce House, 215 South Main, 1892. The hotel was opened in August of 1877 by James and Sarah Pierce. It was sold to James Fitzpatrick in 1880 and a brick addition was added. In 1884, there was diptheria at the Pierce House and the Fitzpatricks tried unsuccessfully to bill the Board of Health $1,100 for damages during closure and disinfection. *Courtesy Olmsted County Historical Society*

Hawthorne School students, 1893. Included are: Ruth Alexander, Irene Franklin Clark, Flora Bliss, Lena Nelson, Herbert Cassaday, Chloe Cooper and Paul Kurtzman. *Courtesy Olmsted County Historical Society*

Tennis club, circa 1895. Included are: C.A. Hutchinson, John Hall, Jim Fairchild, Leslie Stillwell, Frank Justice, Frank Reed and Kirby Halbrook. *Courtesy Olmsted County Historical Society*

Rochester Post Office employees, 1893. Front row, left to right: Lyman Tondro, Postmaster; Lettie Williams, General Delivery Clerk; Florence Tondro Goodrich, Clerk; Ralph Baker, Stampseller; and John Bemis, money order and newspaper stand. In the back row are the first mail carriers who began on January 1, 1891: William Rowley; Arthur Williams; James Jacks and Henry Wrought, sub carrier. The Rochester Post Office was in a building at 1st Avenue S.W. and 2nd Street built in 1875. The building was used as a post office until 1934. *Courtesy Olmsted County Historical Society*

The first team of horses ever used for fire apparatus in Rochester, 1893. Previously, hand carts were used. The team of horses was rented to the Fire Department by Richard Ryan. Left to right: William Murray, William J. Hall, Bill Cudmore, Charles Zimmerman, William Boylhart, Henry (Stony) Jacobs, unidentified, Jack McHugh and Jack Ryan. The electric light plant is to the left and City Hall is on the far left. *Courtesy Olmsted County Historical Society*

Rochester band, circa 1895. Front row, left to right: Ralph Blakely, Art Bach, Fred Allis, William Friedell, Louis Welte, Gene Schwarz, Sr. and Albert Fakler. Middle row: Jack Davis, Lowell Rich, ___ Thorson, Earl W. Wilson and Claude Coon. Top row: Ernest Schlitgus, Sr., Gus Ranfranz, Fred Heyerdale, Will F. Rutz, John Cotterell, Clarence E. Knowlton, John Norton, Axel Thorson and August Fisher. *Courtesy Olmsted County Historical Society*

A pause in the tennis game at Rochester State Hospital, circa 1895. *Courtesy Olmsted County Historical Society*

Sitting room on one of the women's wards at the Rochester State Hospital, circa 1895. *Courtesy Olmsted County Historical Society*

Rochester State Hospital staff tennis team, 1896. *Courtesy Olmsted County Historical Society*

Rochester State Hospital staff, 1896. *Courtesy Olmsted County Historical Society*

Workers at the Oakwood Cemetery, 1896. Left to right: unidentified, Will Hayes, Obi Cummens, Will Nitz and Andrew Holm. *Courtesy Olmsted County Historical Society*

The Cook Hotel at Broadway and 2nd Street S.W., 1898. Built by John R. Cook, the cornerstone for the hotel was laid on July 6, 1869. Because of the depressed wheat market of the 1870s, the hotel remained almost empty except for the first floor offices and businesses. In 1887 John Kahler came to Rochester to manage the Cook Hotel. He redecorated and expanded the hotel from 45 to 100 rooms.making it one of Minnesota finest hotels. The building was razed in 1949. *Courtesy Rochester Post-Bulletin*

Darling Business College, 1896. Built in 1883 by Eugene Young for a school, Rochester Seminary, D. Darling purchased it in 1887 as a home for his business college. The Courthouse can be seen on the left. *Courtesy Olmsted County Historical Society*

Darling Business College graduates, circa 1895, pictured on the Courthouse steps. Professor D. Darling is on the left. Mr. Darling operated a business college in Rochester for many years. His first location was over a downtown store. In 1887 he purchased the Rochester Seminary and moved his college to its new home. He operated the college at that location for 17 years. In 1901 he moved to Fergus Falls where he opened another business college. *Courtesy Olmsted County Historical Society*

John Fulkerson Grocery, 211 S. Broadway, 1896. *Courtesy Olmsted County Historical Society*

Grand Army of the Republic picnic in R.C. Keel's grove, circa 1897. E.A. Knowlton is in the back row on the far left. Others included in the photo are J.A. Leonard, T.H. Bliss, J.H. Wagoner, Sam Miller, Mr. and Mrs. O.T. Dickerman, Harold J. Richardson, C.M. Clough or H.H. Howard, H.M. Richardson, Fred Stroble, Mr. and Mrs. George Stewart, Mrs. Henry Isabler, Mrs. Josephine Seaman, Madge Blethan, Mrs. Kendall, Gertie Stewart Dole, Irene Stewart, Olive Stewart, Maude Seaman Tollefson and Florence Stewart. About 1,250 Olmsted County men fought in the Civil War. Most of them served in Company B of the Second Regiment of Minnesota volunteers which fought in many famous battles and marched with Sherman to the sea. Other Olmsted men served in Company F of the Ninth Regiment and took part in the Sioux uprising in western Minnesota. Another group, Company K of the Third Regiment of Minnesota, was composed largely of Olmsted County men. *Courtesy Olmsted County Historical Society*

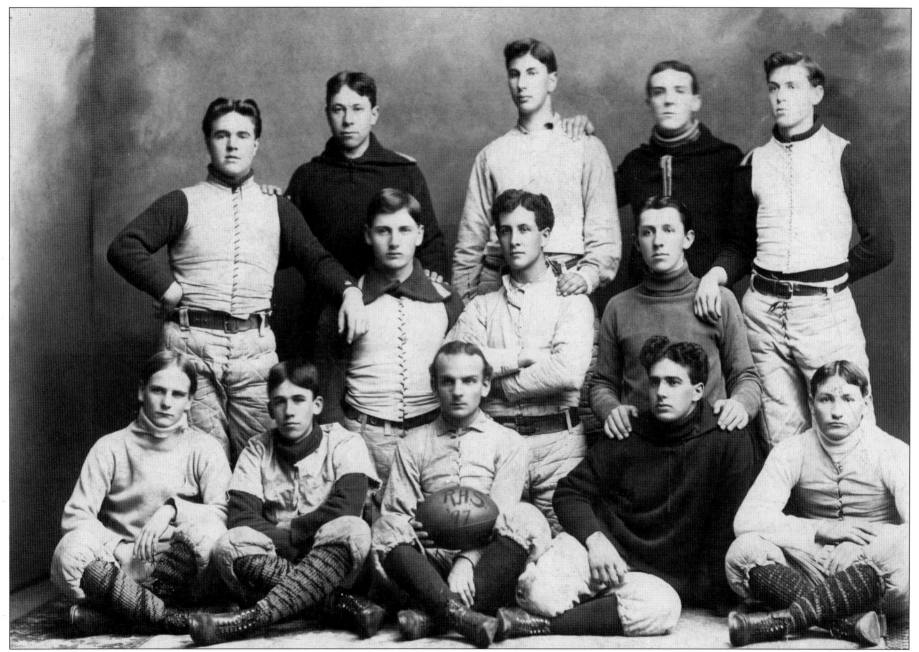

Rochester High School football team, 1897. Standing, left to right: Tom Emerson, Homer Van Campen, George Stevens, Bunn T. Wilson and Major Zickerson. Center row: Frank Madden, Ralph Blethen and Paul Fuller. First row: Neil Judd, Harry Doran, Starr Judd, Herb Cole and Luellington "Louie" Peck. *Courtesy Olmsted County Historical Society*

Dedication of East Center Street Bridge, September 1898. Standing on the bridge are, left to right: Burt W. Eaton, mayor 1893-1899; Joseph Wagoner, former mayor, 1887-1893; Thomas P. Hall; George W. Waldron; Noah B. Wilkins; George J. Allen, city attorney; Clare W. Blakely, alderman; Ole G. Hanson, alderman; H.M. Richardson, sheriff 1881-1893, alderman 1897; J.A. Leonard, Publisher Rochester Post; Will Frazier, contractor; Andrew Madsen, alderman; unknown; Aaron Brown, alderman; and Robert Elliott, city engineer. William Richardson is in the buggy and several painters stood on the sidewalk and on the girders. The bridge cost $12,000 to build. *Courtesy Olmsted County Historical Society*

Poole's Drug Store, 215 S. Broadway, circa 1896. F.A. Poole is on the right; Louis Nietz is on the left. *Courtesy Olmsted County Historical Society*

Mrs. Sanford and Lucy at St. Marys Hospital, April 9, 1898. *Courtesy Olmsted County Historical Society*

Stewartville School, 1899. *Courtesy Olmsted County Historical Society*

First National Bank, Stewartville, circa 1900. The bank closed permanently during the Depression. *Courtesy Olmsted County Historical Society*

A New Century 1900 - 1914

There are few reports of how Rochesterites rang in the 20th century and what their expectations were for the 1900s. But it appears that like in Aesop's fabled Tortoise and Hare, they were looking forward in the new century to slow but steady growth. The population numbered nearly 7,000, hardly a population boom over the preceding nearly 50 years; in 1870, the city's population was about 4,000.

The Mayos' medical practice continued to grow, as did Saint Marys Hospital, which built additions to meet patients' needs.

The Grand Opera House, which had led the entertainment scene in the city, got competition from the construction of the Metropolitan Theater that was built by J. E. Reid on what is now the corner of South Broadway and First Street Southeast. The first movie was shown in Rochester in 1908 and by 1914 film was becoming an entertainment mainstay.

Dr. Charles H. Mayo, who enjoyed mechanics, reportedly owned the first automobile in Rochester, sometime just after the turn of the century. The unpaved streets made motoring an adventure, especially side-by-side with horse-drawn conveyances. The horses frequently demonstrated their fear of the automobiles.

It was war, the Civil War, that brought Dr. William Worrall Mayo to Rochester from Le Sueur as a medical examiner of potential recruits for the army in southern Minnesota. He remained in practice and with his two sons, starting the medical dynasty that would become Mayo Clinic.

Looming in the early part of the century was the War to End All Wars, World War I, and Rochester would not be spared involvement.

Rochester, circa 1900. By the turn of the century Rochester had grown to 6,843. *Courtesy Rochester Post-Bulletin*

A NEW CENTURY 1900-1914

College Street Bridge over the Zumbro River, circa 1900. *Courtesy Olmsted County Historical Society*

Chicago Northwestern engine, circa 1900. The man in dark overalls is Joe Bell. Note the wooden pilot or cow catcher in front. *Courtesy Olmsted County Historical Society*

Rochester High School baseball team, circa 1900. Front row, left to right: Robert J. Schmid, Ray Williamson, ___ Hicks, Alfred Frahm and Frank Gilbert. Middle row: Edgar Gerry and Henry Clemenson. Back row: Walter Parmerlee, ___ McNiff, Frank Morley, Arthur Rueben and Herbert Gilmore. *Courtesy Olmsted County Historical Society*

District #28 "Bear" School, Eyota Township. Cora Hughes is at the head of the line; John Kisro is at the foot. Miss Whited, the teacher, boarded with Esther Mayhood. *Courtesy Olmsted County Historical Society*

Holmes School, circa 1900. *Courtesy Olmsted County Historical Society*

Workers at the State Hospital out for a picnic, circa 1900. Jack Davies is third from the right. *Courtesy Olmsted County Historical Society*

Cussons Flour Mill, Stewartville, circa 1900. *Courtesy Olmsted County Historical Society*

State Hospital Fire Department, circa 1900. *Courtesy Olmsted County Historical Society*

St. Marys Hospital building, circa 1900. St. Marys Hospital opened on October 1, 1889, on 40 acres of land purchased by Dr. W.W. Mayo for the Sisters of St. Francis. The original building was a three-story brick building 40 by 60 feet, with a single private room and three wards. The hospital had 40 beds. It was lighted by oil lamps and there was no telephone system. The first operation was conducted the day the hospital opened. Dr. W.J. Mayo, Dr. C.H. Mayo, with Dr. W.W. Mayo as anesthetist performed a procedure on a malignant lesion of an eye. In 1893, the hospital expanded with a new addition, shown to the left of the original building. The original 1889 building was demolished in 1953. *Courtesy Olmsted County Historical Society*

M.L. Dibble Bicycles shop at 110 W. 4th Street, circa 1900. This became the site of the West Hotel built by Dibble in 1905. *Courtesy Olmsted County Historical Society*

Second grade of Phelps School, 1901. *Courtesy Olmsted County Historical Society*

Dr. Charles Mayo with Mrs. Mayo and Canadian guests pose in a four horsepower Thomas Flyer in 1902. They are pictured at the future site of the Zumbro Hotel. *Courtesy Olmsted County Historical Society*

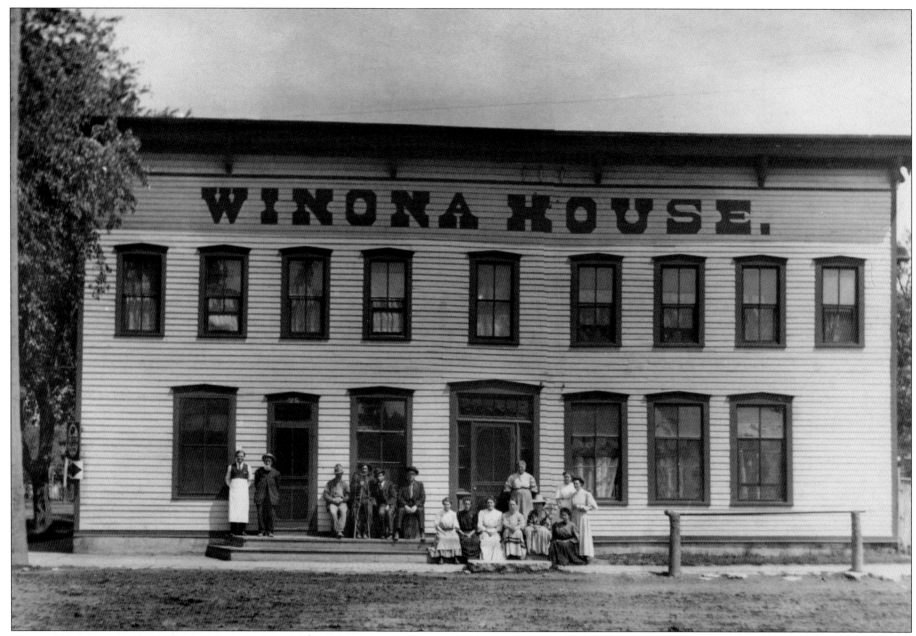

Winona House, circa 1900. The hotel was built in 1869 at the corner of Center Street and 1st Avenue by Robert Smith. It was known for its fine dinners, imported Rhine and catawba wine, and Swiss cheese. The hotel was later owned by Dan J. Sonnenberg who sold it to George Wenting. He sold it to his brother Barney Wenting. Barney Wenting sold it to Charles Grassle who razed it in 1919 and built the Carlton Hotel on the site. Anna M. Wenting is sitting in the center in the light dress. *Courtesy Olmsted County Historical Society*

Pleasant Grove School, circa 1900. Theodore Eppland was the school bus driver. *Courtesy Olmsted County Historical Society*

Dibble Barber Shop, 120 1st Avenue S. W., circa 1900. Jay P. Dibble was the proprietor. The shop was in business from 1898 to 1940. *Courtesy Olmsted County Historical Society*

German Methodist Church near Dover, circa 1905. *Courtesy Olmsted County Historical Society*

Oronoco dam and mill, circa 1902. *Courtesy Olmsted County Historical Society*

Oronoco harness shop, circa 1900. *Courtesy Olmsted County Historical Society*

Pierce Grocery, 109 S. Broadway, circa 1900. J.A. Pierce and Eddie Root are behind the counter. *Courtesy Olmsted County Historical Society*

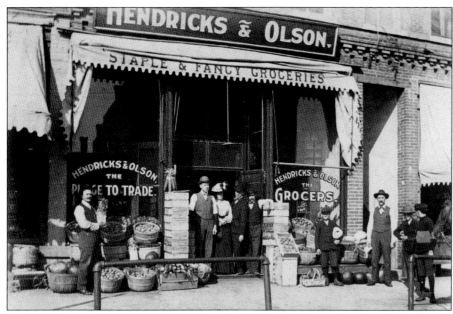

Hendricks & Olson grocery store, 1904. Included are: W.H. Hendricks, August Olson and J.W. Hendricks. *Courtesy Olmsted County Historical Society*

Hawthorne School, 1904. Back row, far left is George Leonard; third from left is Clarence Hanson. Middle row, fourth from right is Florence Currier. Front row, second from right is Walter Alexander; kneeling behind him is Theodore Gray.
Courtesy Olmsted County Historical Society

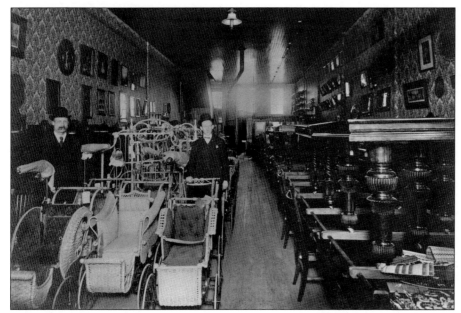

Paine Furniture Company, 313 S. Broadway, 1904. F.J. Paine is on the left. *Courtesy Olmsted County Historical Society*

Rochester Fire Department, 1903. John A. Boylhart was the chief. *Courtesy Olmsted County Historical Society*

The Moon Dry Goods, 1904. *Courtesy Olmsted County Historical Society*

Northrup School, North Rochester, was built in 1875 and razed in 1915. *Courtesy Olmsted County Historical Society*

State Hospital staff baseball team, circa 1905. Clayton Renslow is seated second from the left. *Courtesy Olmsted County Historical Society*

District #103 Fogarty School, circa 1905. Front row, left to right: Monte Pearson, Bernice Johnson, Marjorie O'Connell, Cora Eserman and Paul Joslyn. Included in middle row: Scott Jenkins, Francis O'Connell, Pine Eserman, Loretta St. George, Earl Eserman, Carl Joslyn and Howard Joslyn. Back row: Mary Thompson, Bert Nicholas, Myra Pearson, Lilie Eserman and Agnes St. George. *Courtesy Olmsted County Historical Society*

A NEW CENTURY 1900-1914

S. Broadway looking toward the old Central Fire Station, 1905. *Courtesy Olmsted County Historical Society*

Fourth of July on Broadway, 1902. *Courtesy Olmsted County Historical Society*

A NEW CENTURY 1900-1914

Rochester High School baseball team, 1906. Back row, left to right: Gerry, Budde, Overholt, Fitzgerald, Malone, Dr. Berkman, Lawler and Oldsworth. Second row: Berkman, McQuillen, mascot Whited, Abersvold and Pollack. Front: McDermott and Hall. *Courtesy Olmsted County Historical Society*

The Zumbro River rose 18 feet and flooded parts of Rochester on June 23, 1908. Mayo Park was submerged and water flowed down Dubuque Street (3rd Avenue S.E.) for the first time in Rochester history. It was the worst flood in the city's history at that time. *Courtesy Olmsted County Historical Society*

Bridge north of Stewartville, circa 1905. *Courtesy Olmsted County Historical Society*

Ruins of W.S. Davis Hardware Store, Stewartville, July 11, 1909. *Courtesy Olmsted County Historical Society*

1908 graduates of the Rochester State Hospital Nursing School. Back row, left to right: Earl Pomeroy, Ira Gaskill, Alfreda Tomsen, Miss Gordon, Dr. Linton, Wilhelmena Drews and Ina Boslough. Middle row: Dr. Hejesdale, Dr. Kilbourne, Dr. Phelps and Dr. Chapple. Front row: Ethel Van Camp, Ella Nichols, Ellen Gregory, Bertha Jensen and Anna Taylor. *Courtesy Olmsted County Historical Society*

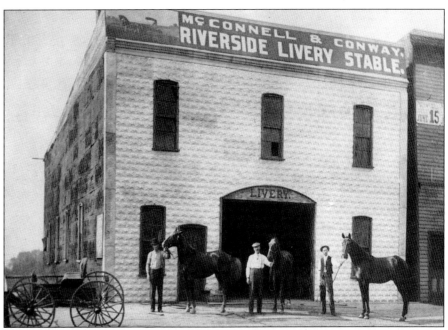

Riverside Livery Stable, circa 1908. *Courtesy Olmsted County Historical Society*

The Academy of Our Lady of Lourdes, which served as motherhouse for the Sisters of Saint Francis, stood on W. Center Street from 1877 to 1955. *Courtesy Olmsted County Historical Society*

H.A. Johnson Barbershop, Dover, 1909. *Courtesy Olmsted County Historical Society*

J.G. Bush home, Dover, circa 1910. *Courtesy Olmsted County Historical Society*

One of the earliest Kahler hotel-hospitals was the former E.A. Knowlton house. Dry goods businessman E.A. Knowlton, Dr. Christopher Graham and J.H. Kahler converted the house into a sanatorium and outpatient lodgings in 1907. Besides its oriental rugs and brass beds it featured an operating room. It became the Hotel Damon in 1921. *Courtesy Rochester Post-Bulletin*

Rock Dell Township gathering, circa 1910. Front row, fourth and fifth from the right are Mr. and Mrs. Gilbertson. Second row, tall middle lady in the striped dress is ___ Gilbertson. Back row on the right is Albert Gilbertson.
Courtesy Olmsted County Historical Society

Simpson School, 1907. *Courtesy Olmsted County Historical Society*

Grimm's Meat Market, circa 1908. Included in the picture are: Clara Sawinski, Hugh Nichols, Art Schlitgus, Charles Grimm, Otto Kiecker and Hank Witzke. *Courtesy Olmsted County Historical Society*

Main Street, Dover, circa 1910. Buildings, left to right: Coal sheds, unknown, Dover Independent newspaper, First State Bank, Charles Bush Drygoods, grocery and drug store of J.G. Bush and a barber shop. The Dover Independent was a monthly newspaper in 1891 and in 1905 Ernest Eckles established it as a weekly. *Courtesy Olmsted County Historical Society*

Boating on Lake Florence near Stewartville, circa 1910. *Courtesy Olmsted County Historical Society*

Methodist Episcopal Church, Dover, was built in 1876. Reverend M.O. McNiff was the first minister. *Courtesy Olmsted County Historical Society*

Grunger's Hunting Lodge, Kalmar Township, circa 1910. *Courtesy Olmsted County Historical Society*

A NEW CENTURY 1900-1914

Rochester Mill, circa 1910. *Courtesy Olmsted County Historical Society*

Rochester baseball club, circa 1910. *Courtesy Olmsted County Historical Society*

Rochester High School girls basketball team, circa 1910. *Courtesy Olmsted County Historical Society*

"Old Mill Dam" in Oronoco, circa 1910. *Courtesy Olmsted County Historical Society*

Christmas in the State Hospital Day Room, circa 1910. Nurses are Farnum, Larson, Skyhawk and Hanson. *Courtesy Olmsted County Historical Society*

A NEW CENTURY 1900-1914

The station was established by Winona & St. Peter Railroad in 1869 and named Dover Center. In 1874, the grain elevator was built by Fairfield Smith. *Courtesy Olmsted County Historical Society*

The Dover School was built around 1876. *Courtesy Olmsted County Historical Society*

Dr. Plummer's cottage on Lake Shady, Oronoco, circa 1910. Dr. Plummer came to the Mayo Clinic in 1901. Many wealthy Rochester families had cottages on Lake Shady and spent part of their summers there. *Courtesy Olmsted County Historical Society*

Monogram Bar at 214 S. Broadway, circa 1910. Charlie Kruesel was the proprietor. *Courtesy Olmsted County Historical Society*

Rochester Fire Department, 1911. In the wagon at left holding the reins is Chief John Boylhart. Other firemen include: Eugene Schwarz, William Cudmore, J.A. Pierce and Ed Hicks. *Courtesy Olmsted County Historical Society*

A NEW CENTURY 1900-1914

The Rochester Public Library was built in 1898 on the corner of 2nd Street and 1st Avenue S. W. It served as the library until 1937 and was razed in 1948.
Courtesy Olmsted County Historical Society

Rochester baseball club, 1910. *Courtesy Olmsted County Historical Society*

Central School building on fire, September 1, 1910. The building was constructed with locally-made bricks in 1867-68. It continued to be used as a grade school until 1926. *Courtesy Olmsted County Historical Society*

Chicago Great Western Depot, 1911. The Chicago and Great Western Railway Company built a line from Rochester to Zumbrota in 1902. The line was extended to Red Wing and then to St. Paul. For many years this was the only railroad line from the Twin Cities which came to Rochester without a transfer. The trip from Rochester to the Twin Cities took about five hours. *Courtesy Olmsted County Historical Society*

Fire Chief John Boylhart, Ed Hicks, Jack McHugh and Dick Ryan in front of Central Station, circa 1911. *Courtesy Olmsted County Historical Society*

Carving the ox, Stewartville, October 1, 1913. Ed Stokye is in the foreground in the long white coat. Others, left to right: ___ McGrath, Ed Hall, Homer Wooldridge, John Brooks in center in white coat, John Towey and Henry Ringly. *Courtesy Olmsted County Historical Society*

A NEW CENTURY 1900-1914

Rochester High School 1913 basketball team. *Courtesy Olmsted County Historical Society*

First Baptist Church fire, March 9, 1912. The first motorized fire engine was used in 1912, sending streams of water into the fire. *Courtesy Olmsted County Historical Society*

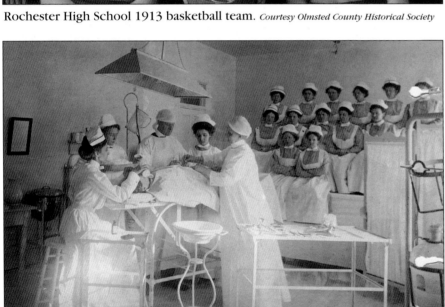
Operating room at the Rochester State Hospital, circa 1910. *Courtesy Olmsted County Historical Society*

Students at Hadley Valley School, 1914. *Courtesy Olmsted County Historical Society*

THE WAR YEARS 1914 - 1945

Rochester was not spared the years of upheaval and hardship that marked the generation that lived between the beginning of World War I and the end of World War II. Rochester mothers sent their sons to the battlefields in France in 1917 and again to Europe and the Pacific theaters of war only a quarter century later. Many did not return.

The citizens celebrated the defeat of the Kaiser in 1918 and welcomed the local Doughboys back home. Then the Twenties roared in and "23 skidoo, I love my wife but oh you kid," became the Thirties when the song was "Brother, Can You Spare a Dime."

During WWII, 1941 to 1945, citizens joined their neighbors in saving newspapers and string and aluminum foil. Gold Stars appeared in the windows of Rochester houses when a son or daughter was lost to war. Just about everything was rationed. There were two pork chops on the dinner table for a family of four. You could get enough gasoline to get to work, if you were careful, but rubber tires were doctored with patch after patch because they were needed for the war effort. Even newsprint and flashbulbs were rationed. War Bond drives brought in money needed for the war effort. And Rosie the Riveter went to work helping the boys overseas fighting for freedom.

Rochester didn't stand still. Mayo Clinic continued to treat a growing number of patients and visitors continued to come to the city. The Kahler Hotel was built in 1920 and Mayo Clinic opened the Plummer Building in 1928. To meet the need for nurses, the Methodist Kahler School of Nursing was opened and Saint Marys continued to train nurses. The Chateau Theatre opened in 1938. Folks were entertained at the new Mayo Civic Auditorium, donated by the Mayo brothers to the city in 1939, the auditorium a venue for sports, music and ice reviews.

Automobiles and taxi cabs replaced horse and buggies and hitching posts disappeared from Broadway. Independence Day was celebrated with flags, parades and a good old summertime. Names that still can be heard were put on buildings and businesses — Newton Hollands Cafeteria and the Princess Cafe, Nelson Tire and Rochester Dairy.

Weather was its usual concern, except for the Armistice Day blizzard of November 11, 1940, that caused several deaths.

With the soldiers home from war after VJ day in 1945, Rochester settled into a period of peace and prosperity when the city and its institutions began its post-war growth spurt.

Unveiling the W.W. Mayo monument in Mayo Park, May 29, 1915. *Courtesy Olmsted County Historical Society*

THE WAR YEARS 1915-1945

Nelson Motor Sales greasing station, 1st Avenue S. W., circa 1915. *Courtesy Olmsted County Historical*

The West Hotel was built in 1905 by M.L. Dibble at 110-112 W. 4th Street (1st Street S. W.), the site formally occupied by his bike shop and blacksmith shop. He later sold the hotel to the Kahler Corporation. Mr. Dibble is standing in front of the hotel, 1917. *Courtesy Olmsted County Historical Society*

Post Office workers, 1916. Seated, left to right: James L. Matheson, Mary Sweeney, D.L. Williams and Howard Mulholland. Standing: James Jacks, Reed Haggerty, Tal Williams, Jr., Frank Lyons, Henry Wrought, Art Graham and William Rowley. The boy, Harry Rowley, ran errands for the group. *Courtesy Olmsted County Historical Society*

Hawthorne School, 1917. *Courtesy Olmsted County Historical Society*

Mayo Dental building, circa 1915. *Courtesy Olmsted County Historical Society*

Mayo Clinic 1914 building. *Courtesy Olmsted County Historical Society*

Construction of the Rochester Power Dam, 1919. *Courtesy Olmsted County Historical Society*

THE WAR YEARS 1915-1945

Interior of the Chicago Northwestern depot, March 28, 1919. *Courtesy Olmsted County Historical Society*

Picnic for Mayo Clinic X-ray department at Fugel's Mill, southeast of Simpson, 1920. Left to right: unknown, Sam T. Hutton, William J. Arrasmith, Dr. Clement L. Martin, Dr. Charles G. Sutherland, Dr. J.C. Brogden, Desmond Vallely, Dr. J.W. Pangburn and Dr. A.U. Desjardines. Seated: Gene Taylor and Dr. Russell D. Carmen. *Courtesy Olmsted County Historical Society*

Bridge at Oronoco shortly after it was built, circa 1920. *Courtesy Olmsted County Historical Society*

Rochester street scene, circa 1920. *Courtesy Olmsted County Historical Society*

Construction of the Kahler Hotel, 1920, looking from the Post Office. The building was done by Garfield Schwartz of Rochester, who also built the 1914 and 1929 Mayo Clinic buildings. *Courtesy Rochester Post-Bulletin*

Rochester 1920 High School football team. Included are: Glenn Amundsen, F. Stewart, Kenneth Abernathy, Henry Maas, Floyd Hill, Henry Kalb, Donald Taylor, Fay Alexander, Max Kjerner, Walter Thompson, Harold Hasse, Clifford Alexander, Coach Fredericks, Nemo Weinholdt, Oscar Studenruth, Emil Ludtke, Malcolm Chapman, Gordon Graham and Glenn Fordham. *Courtesy Olmsted County Historical Society*

Methodist Kahler School of Nursing, circa 1920. The school was formed in 1918 as the Colonial and Allied Hospitals Training School for Nurses to help meet the nursing shortages of World War I. It was later called Kahler, then Methodist-Kahler. The group is assembled in front of The Colonial Hospital. *Courtesy Olmsted County Historical Society*

Holmes School, a public elementary school constructed in 1920. *Courtesy Olmsted County Historical Society*

Dodge Lumber & Fuel Company, built in 1916 by Elam P. Dodge. *Courtesy Olmsted County Historical Society*

Zumbro Hotel, 1920. The hotel was built in 1912 at the corner of 1st Avenue and 1st Street S. W. by the Zumbro Hotel Corporation which was composed of J.H. Kahler, Dr. C. Graham and George Weber. It had a three floor bridge in connection with the Mayo Clinic which sat directly at its rear. The Chicago and Great Western railroad uptown ticket office was in the lobby. *Courtesy Olmsted County Historical Society*

First Kahler Hotel kitchen crew, 1921. Chef Henri Bakker is on the left. *Courtesy Rochester Post-Bulletin*

Oesterreich Billiards, Bowling Alley, and Barber Shop, 9 S. Broadway, 1921. The business was owned by Fred and Anna Oestrerreich. *Courtesy Olmsted County Historical Society*

Interior of the Hotel Kahler lobby as it looked when it opened in 1921. *Courtesy Rochester Post-Bulletin*

Post Office employees, October 1925. Front row, from left: Earl Tesca, Joe Wegman, Art Schmitt, Vern Rahm, Chauncy Durand, James Matheson, D.L. Williams, P.M. Frank Schmelzer, Louis Allen and Arthur Carroll. Center row: William Sawinski, John Knutzen, Archie Lawler, Lester Spring, Clarence Stewart, Cephas Palmer, Loren Moeller, Edward Blattner and Ross Johnson. Back row: Franklin Buller, Judge Callaghan, Russell Farnham, Art Knutzen, John Harms, Howard Saunders, Patrick Condron, Floyd Wilkins and Julius Jacobson. *Courtesy Olmsted County Historical Society*

St. Marys class of nurses and Sister, 1927. *Courtesy Olmsted County Historical Society*

Workroom at the Rochester Post Office on the southeast corner of 1st Avenue and 1st Street S. W., circa 1925. *Courtesy Olmsted County Historical Society*

The Princess Cafe, circa 1925. *Courtesy Olmsted County Historical Society*

Olmsted County eighth grade graduating class of 1924. *Courtesy Olmsted County Historical Society*

THE WAR YEARS 1915-1945

Rochester's first swim team, 1925. Included are: Coach V.J. Baatz, William Aune, Jim Malone, David Quale, Bill Hyerdale, Hawley Sanford, Charles Truax, Noel Ashworth, George Matheson, Bruce Matheson and Fred Helmholtz. *Courtesy Olmsted County Historical Society*

St. Marys Hospital diet kitchen, 1924. Margaret South was the dietician at this time. *Courtesy Olmsted County Historical Society*

Home Oil Company, 1301 N. Broadway, circa 1924. *Courtesy Olmsted County Historical Society*

Ford Automobiles being delivered at Motor Sales & Service, 1928. *Courtesy Olmsted County Historical Society*

Empress Billiards, 1926. Included are: Hugh "Tubby" Bay, Frank Frifer, Bill Miller and Elmer Roster. *Courtesy Olmsted County Historical Society*

Parade in downtown Rochester, circa 1929. *Courtesy Rochester Post-Bulletin*

CELEBRATING 150 YEARS

Post Office on the corner of 1st Avenue and 1st Street S. W. was in use from 1912-1934 and was razed in 1939 once the new building was built. *Courtesy Olmsted County Historical Society*

Folwell School, located at 6th Street and 15th Avenue, was built in 1930. An addition was built in 1950. *Courtesy Olmsted County Historical Society*

Adding the carillon to the top of the Plummer Building, 1928. The 19-story building took over as the major Mayo Clinic building. The 56-bell carillon was added and dedicated to the soldiers of World War I. *Courtesy Olmsted County Historical Society*

THE WAR YEARS 1915-1945

Hollands Cafeteria and Food Shop, 2105 Broadway, opened as a grocery store in 1907 and was owned by Ernest Holland and William Campbell. In 1925 a small bakery and catering service was added. Ernest's son, Newton, took over the business in 1927 and moved it in 1930 to 216 1st Avenue S.W. In 1944 it became a restaurant which was in business until 1970. *Courtesy Olmsted County Historical Society*

Mayowood, circa 1930. Mayowood, built in 1910, was the home of Dr. Charles Mayo. The 40-room home featured extensive gardens and a private lake. *Courtesy Olmsted County Historical Society*

Air mail service began in Rochester on March 8, 1930. Left to right: Northwest pilot; E.H. Schlitgus, president of Rochester Commercial Club (RCC); A.J. Lobb, past RCC vice-president and chairman of Rochester Airport Commission; Ruby Clark, Northwest representative; D.L. Williams, past RCC president and Rochester Postmaster; Dyer H. Campbell, RCC secretary; and Northwest pilot. *Courtesy Olmsted County Historical Society*

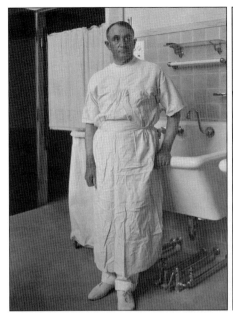 

Dr. Charles Horace Mayo, Dr. Charlie, and Dr. William James Mayo, Dr. Will, in their "working clothes," circa 1930. *Courtesy Olmsted County Historical Society*

Riding in an open air car are, left to right: U.S. President Franklin D. Roosevelt, Dr. Charles Mayo and Dr. William Mayo, 1934. The President was in Rochester to join the American Legion in honoring the Mayo brothers for their work in caring for disabled veterans. *Courtesy Olmsted County Historical Society*

Nelson Tire Service basketball team, 1931-32, S.E. Minnesota District Champions. *Courtesy Olmsted County Historical Society*

Delivery men and trucks for Rochester Dairy, circa 1935. *Courtesy Olmsted County Historical Society*

Nelson Tire Service, circa 1935. The building at S. Broadway and 4th Street S. E. was built in 1917 by the Olmsted County Cooperative Association for a general store which closed around 1922. *Courtesy Olmsted County Historical Society*

Stewartville High School basketball team, March 1935. *Courtesy Olmsted County Historical Society*

Rochester Dairy, circa 1935. The building at 4th Street and 1st Avenue S. W. was formerly the Schuster Brewery. *Courtesy Olmsted County Historical Society*

Rochester Bottling Company, circa 1938. *Courtesy Olmsted County Historical Society*

Boxing team for Motor Sales and Service, circa 1935. *Courtesy Olmsted County Historical Society*

Edison School, 1931. *Courtesy Olmsted County Historical Society*

Hanson Hardware Company with a freight carload of Frigidaires arriving March 4, 1937. *Courtesy Olmsted County Historical Society*

District #67 Skyline or Bigelow School, 1936-37. Front row, left to right: Charles Roller, Lenore Martig, Phyllis Sykes, Marjorie Steiger, Marie Kohlmeyer and Bernita Day. Middle row: Melvin "Jack" Day, Donna Kohlmeyer, Anna Rupkalvis, Lorraine Day, Mary Ann Roller and Luella Kohlmeyer. Back row is unidentified. *Courtesy Olmsted County Historical Society*

Parade in front of the Chateau Theater, 1938. *Courtesy Olmsted County Historical Society*

Cooking class at the Chateau Theater, May 1, 1936. *Courtesy Olmsted County Historical Society*

Stained glass at St. Marys, circa 1940. *Courtesy Olmsted County Historical Society*

Rochester Junior College football team, 1939. *Courtesy Olmsted County Historical Society*

Stewartville Fire Department, 1939. *Courtesy Olmsted County Historical Society*

Motor Sales and Service, a Ford dealership, 1938. Joy Brothers Packard Sales and Service is on the right and Rochester Dairy Company is in the background. *Courtesy Olmsted County Historical Society*

The Post Office was located at the corner of 1st Street and 3rd Avenue S. W. from 1934 to 1969. *Courtesy Olmsted County Historical Society*

Rochester High School basketball team, 1939. *Courtesy Olmsted County Historical Society*

Priebe Cabins Deluxe Cabin Court, circa 1940. The cabins and apartments were located at the junction of highways 52 and 14 on the west side of Rochester. *Courtesy Olmsted County Historical Society*

Nursery at St. Marys Hospital, circa 1940. *Courtesy Olmsted County Historical Society*

Digging out from the Armistice Day storm, November 11, 1940. The unexpected storm claimed the lives of many Minnesotans. *Courtesy Rochester Post-Bulletin*

Olmsted County School Patrol, 1941-42. *Courtesy Olmsted County Historical Society*

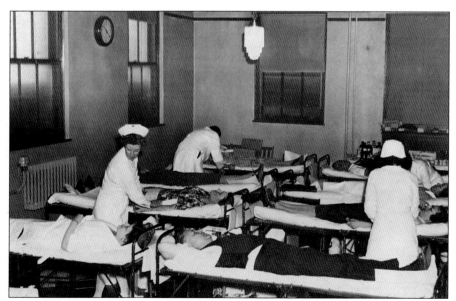

Red Cross Bloodmobile at City Hall, December 20, 1943. *Courtesy Olmsted County Historical Society*

THE WAR YEARS 1915-1945

War bonds being sold at Knowlton's Store, September 17, 1942. *Courtesy Olmsted County Historical Society*

Three mothers of sons in the military service overseas mailing Christmas gifts to their boys, 1943. Being helped by clerk Robert Campbell are Mrs. Fred Walbruch, Mrs. Clarence W. Higbie and Mrs. P.R. Tierne. *Courtesy Olmsted County Historical Society*

Christening of the 45-foot navy picket boat sponsored by war bond purchases of the people of Rochester and Olmsted County. Eileen Meadows, 14, broke the bottle of champagne on the bow of the vessel as the craft began its launch at Shain Manufacturing Company Shipyard in Seattle, July 17, 1943. Representing the thirteenth naval district was Lieutenant Commander L.H. Hirschy. *Courtesy Olmsted County Historical Society*

Stewartville parade, August 14, 1945, celebrating Victory Over Japan (VJ Day). *Courtesy Olmsted County Historical Society*

Celebrating Victory Over Japan (VJ Day) in Rochester, August 14, 1945. *Courtesy Rochester Post-Bulletin*

The Rochester Post-Bulletin proclaims the surrender of Japan as a crowd gathers to celebrate Victory Over Japan, August 14, 1945. *Courtesy Rochester Post-Bulletin*

Stewartville parade celebrating Victory Over Japan Day (VJ Day), August 14, 1945. *Courtesy Olmsted County Historical Society*

Peace & Prosperity 1946 - 1977

Post-war Rochester settled down to quietly go about its business. Older residents will remember this generation as having few major interruptions in their lives — there was the Zumbro River flood of 1951 which set southeast Rochester awash and the Korean Conflict. But all in all, it was a time of growth, commerce and living life a quality city provided.

Downtown was Dayton's, Montgomery Wards, Sears, J.C. Penney, Woolworth's and a slew of smaller stores. The first large shopping center outside of the Twin Cities, Miracle Mile, opened in 1952. Apache Mall opened in 1969 with 39 stores, the first enclosed mall in southeastern Minnesota. IBM opened its sixth major U.S. plant in 1958 in a farm field in northwest Rochester with a promise to become an economic competitor to Mayo Clinic.

Commercial airliners hauled patients and visitors to the city along with a procession of celebrities, including princes and presidents. The airport, in southeast Rochester, was moved south to accommodate a needed larger facility. The growth of air travel heralded the demise of passenger rail travel here and the last Chicago & Northwestern passenger train pulled into Rochester in 1963.

Mayo was not standing still. The new $25 million Mayo Building was added to the downtown skyline in 1953 and expanded to 19 floors in 1969.

The *Post-Bulletin*, the city's only daily newspaper, celebrated its 25th anniversary in 1950 and that technological wonder, TV, came as KROC, Channel 10, began broadcasting in 1958.

By the 1970s, the downtown was beginning to look a little shabby and plans were drawn to use federal urban renewal funds to redevelop the core downtown. But opposition to the plan killed the program and the city had to wait for private investment to spruce it up.

Birdseye view of downtown Rochester, circa 1946. *Courtesy Rochester Post-Bulletin*

Crowd of shoppers at the F. Massey Company, circa 1946. *Courtesy Olmsted County Historical Society*

Rochester Blue Socks baseball team, 1947. *Courtesy Olmsted County Historical Society*

Cook Hotel fire, February 5, 1946. The building, built in 1869, was the first hotel in Rochester managed by John Kahler. With its high-ceilinged rooms, white marble fireplaces, and beautiful long corridors, the Cook Hotel was known to people from all parts of the world. In its early days it was said to be the finest hotel in southern Minnesota. The building was demolished in 1949. *Courtesy Olmsted County Historical Society*

Boxer Joe Lewis fought in Rochester, January 19, 1949. *Courtesy Rochester Post-Bulletin*

Looking toward the Mayo Clinic with the Hotel Damon on the right, 1950. The Mayo brothers maintained an operating room in the hotel for several years. The Methodist Kahler School of Nursing also used part of the hotel for many years for student housing, offices, and classrooms. The building was gutted by fire in 1960 while being demolished to make a parking lot. *Courtesy Olmsted County Historical Society*

This building, on the northeast corner of Broadway and Zumbro, was built in 1876 by C.H. Chadbourn and originally occupied by A.T. Stebbins Hardware. In 1894, it became the Queen City Restaurant which operated until 1938. Jerry's Bar occupied it from 1938 until 1949 when the building was razed and a new building was built for O'Connor's Mens Store. *Courtesy Olmsted County Historical Society*

CELEBRATING 150 YEARS

1st Avenue S. W. looking north, circa 1950. *Courtesy Olmsted County Historical Society*

Claton Hotel, 1950. The hotel was built in 1915 by J. Crabb at 215 W. 5th Street. *Courtesy Olmsted County Historical Society*

Floodwaters at the Rochester Dairy Co-op during the 1951 flood on July 21. The Zumbro River crested at 17.5 feet, the sixth highest crest in the river's history. *Courtesy Rochester Post-Bulletin*

Opening of Donaldson's Department Store in Miracle Mile, October 1953. *Courtesy Olmsted County Historical Society*

West side of 1st Avenue S.W. looking north taken from the intersection of 3rd Street and 1st Avenue. Pictured are: Rubensteins furniture store, Lawler Theater, Model Laundry, First National Bank, and across 2nd Street are the Masonic Temple and Zumbro Hotel. Picture was taken in June 1954 during Rochester's Centennial. The tower of the 1928 clinic tops all the other buildings. *Courtesy Olmsted County Historical Society*

CELEBRATING 150 YEARS

Main entrance to St. Marys Hospital, June 1954. *Courtesy Olmsted County Historical Society*

Montgomery Ward store in downtown Rochester, circa 1955. *Courtesy Rochester Post-Bulletin*

IBM Open House, October 1956. The Rochester facility was IBM's sixth major plant in the United States. *Courtesy Rochester Post-Bulletin*

District #100 Haverhill School, circa 1955. *Courtesy Olmsted County Historical Society*

PEACE & PROSPERITY 1946-1977

U.S. President Dwight D. Eisenhower speaks at the airport during a visit to Rochester in the 1950s. During his stop he also visited polio patients at St. Marys Hospital. *Courtesy Rochester Post-Bulletin*

Harriet Bishop school children crossing the street, circa 1955. *Courtesy Olmsted County Historical Society*

Public Library, 226 2nd Street S.W., was used as the library from 1937-1972. It then became a student center for the Mayo Clinic. Photo is circa 1955. *Courtesy Olmsted County Historical Society*

Miracle Mile Shopping Center, November 8, 1958. The center, built in 1952, was the largest of its kind outside the Twin Cities. *Courtesy Rochester Post-Bulletin*

J.C. Penney store fire, November 17 and 18, 1956. *Courtesy Rochester Post-Bulletin*

Fire sale following the J.C. Penney store fire, December 20, 1956. *Courtesy Rochester Post-Bulletin*

F.W. Woolworth store and Dayton's, circa 1960. Dayton's opened on March 4, 1954, and was the first Dayton's outside of Minneapolis. *Courtesy Olmsted County Historical Society*

#519, the west bound Chicago Northwestern "400" pulls into the Rochester station for the last time, July 23, 1963. *Courtesy Olmsted County Historical Society*

PEACE & PROSPERITY 1946-1977

Richard and Pat Nixon's visit to Rochester, September 19, 1960. *Courtesy Rochester Post-Bulletin*

Apache Mall opened in 1969 with 39 stores. It was the first enclosed mall in southeastern Minnesota. *Courtesy Rochester Post-Bulletin*

Sister Mary Brigh, St. Marys' administrator from 1949, standing beside the statue of Edith Graham Mayo, Rochester's first trained nurse, September 23, 1964. *Courtesy Olmsted County Historical Society*

100 1st Avenue, circa 1965. KROC, channel 10, began broadcasting the first locally originated TV programs on July 16, 1958. *Courtesy Olmsted County Historical Society*

U.S. Supreme Court Justice Harry Blackman addresses a crowd at the Kahler Hotel for a celebration honoring him, August 13, 1970. Justice Blackman, who lived in Rochester from 1950 to 1970, served on the Supreme Court for 24 years. *Courtesy Rochester Post-Bulletin*

John Marshall State High School basketball champions, 1969. Front row, left to right: Tom Zackery, Kraig Wold, Dave Hollander, Mark Hanson, Tom Senst, Craig Jensen and Paul Stillwell. Back row: Head Coach Al Wold, Assistant Coach Dave Grimsrud, Steve Johnson, Ken Lear, Mark Winholtz, Bob Burfeind, Tom Polt, Manager Jim Fisk and Athletic Director Kerwin Engelhart. *Courtesy Olmsted County Historical Society*

A $25 million Mayo Clinic building expansion added to the Rochester skyline in 1969. The Plummer building is on the right. *Courtesy Olmsted County Historical Society*

Fire at the Miracle Mile Shopping Center on February 21, 1971, caused $1.5 million in damage and gutted 26 stores and offices. More than 40 firemen fought the fire, the worst in Rochester's history at that time. *Courtesy Rochester Post-Bulletin*

Kindergarten class of Oronoco School, 1975-76. Included are: Teacher Mrs. Stenson, Robert Haglund, Terry Pettey, Timothy Higgins, Connie Rueber, Beth Ann Templeton, Bonnie Hareldson, Ari Beedle, Karen Andrew, Scott Tiede, Michael Bowlus and Karen Jansen. *Courtesy Olmsted County Historical Society*

Central Junior High School in Rochester, November 1977. *Courtesy Rochester Post-Bulletin*

Flood & Redevelopment 1978 - 1999

When you live in the bottom of a bowl with four rivers and creeks running through it, it stands to reason you can expect a flood. One, in 1857, took out bridges over the Zumbro River and Bear Creek. As the city developed, flood damage was multiplied. The flood of 1908 crested at 18 feet but there wasn't much to wash away. Each spring and summer through the 1950s, '60s and '70s the waters crested, sometimes two or three times in a single year.

It was July 5, 1978, when rains, pounding a saturated ground started falling after an Independence Day celebration, ran off to crest the Zumbro River at 23 feet, taking five lives and causing millions of dollars in damages. After 19 floods in 27 years, this 100-year occurrence galvanized the city into action. Not only was flood control on the agenda, but expansion of Mayo Civic Auditorium that was swamped by flood waters. City leaders were also looking for a private redevelopment of the downtown after urban renewal failed.

Where Mayo Clinic construction had been the rule over the years and continues even today, the skyline was also topped by cranes doing the $44 million downtown remodeling that included a hotel, office complex, shopping mall and skyways. Downtown reconstruction was needed, in part, because the large retailers that had anchored the downtown had moved to shopping centers on the then-southern edge of the city.

Besides building, the 1980s and 1990s were a period of rapid population growth, bringing the city's population in 2002 to 89,325 people — making it the third largest city in the state. And the city's population has diversified. Rochester's foreign-born population is somewhere around 5 percent, with more than 62 percent immigrating in the last decade. The ethnic groups include Latinos, Asians and Africans and Eastern European natives.

Although the influx of foreign-born residents has slowed since September 11, 2001, immigration is expected to be a factor in the city's growth and labor force in the new millennium.

Water surrounded the Silver Lake Power Plant during the flood of 1978. Rains that began July 5 caused the Zumbro River to flood large areas of Rochester before it crested at a record 23 feet, 11 feet above flood stage. Five thousand homes were evacuated after storm clouds had dumped nearly seven inches of rain. There was $75 million in damage. *Courtesy Rochester Post-Bulletin*

FLOOD & REDEVELOPMENT 1978-1999

Floodwaters at an apartment house at 3rd Avenue and 3rd Street S.E. during the 1978 flood. *Courtesy Rochester Post-Bulletin*

A boat motors past Dison's Laundry on 12th Street S.E. during the 1978 flood. *Courtesy Rochester Post-Bulletin*

Volunteers helped rescue people near the Tropic Bowl in southeast Rochester during the 1978 flood. The Tropic Bowl was later demolished as part of the city's flood control project. *Courtesy Rochester Post-Bulletin*

Flood waters reach their crest at the Red Owl store in the Northbrook Shopping Center, July 1978. *Courtesy Rochester Post-Bulletin*

Rochester residents walked through waist-high water in a Rochester street caused by the rains that forced Bear Creek, the Zumbro River, and other streams in the area out of their banks, flooding large areas of the city, July 1978. *Courtesy Rochester Post-Bulletin*

The 1978 flood submerged K-Mart on 3rd Avenue S.E. *Courtesy Rochester Post-Bulletin*

Rochester firefighters patrolled the Zumbro River around the Mayo statues behind the Civic Center during the 1978 flood. *Courtesy Rochester Post-Bulletin*

Floodwaters flow through Rochester during the 1978 flood. It started raining during the evening of July 5. Before the rains stopped nearly seven inches had fallen, causing the worst flooding in Rochester history and leading to major redevelopment, including the largest flood control project ever built by the Army Corps of Engineers in the upper Midwest. *Courtesy Rochester Post-Bulletin*

Rochester celebrates the reopening of the J.C. Penney store in the Apache Mall, September, 1984, after it had undergone a complete remodeling. The store had been in the mall since the Apache Mall opened in 1969 after being in downtown Rochester for many years. *Courtesy Rochester Post-Bulletin*

The "Family of Man" reliefs on the Mayo Clinic Building, 1985. The Plummer Building is on the right. *Courtesy Rochester Post-Bulletin*

Broadway and 4th Street, June 27, 1985. *Courtesy Rochester Post-Bulletin*

Feeding the geese at Silver Lake, circa 1985. One theory is the Giant Canada geese were originally brought to Rochester by Dr. Charlie Mayo. Their numbers grew from about 500 in 1949 to more than 33,000 in 1983 when the goose was incorporated as the symbol of Rochester's 125th anniversary. *Courtesy Rochester Post-Bulletin*

Aerial view of the Sisters of St. Francis Motherhouse on Assisi Heights in northwest Rochester, 1986. The facility was built in 1955. *Courtesy Rochester Post-Bulletin*

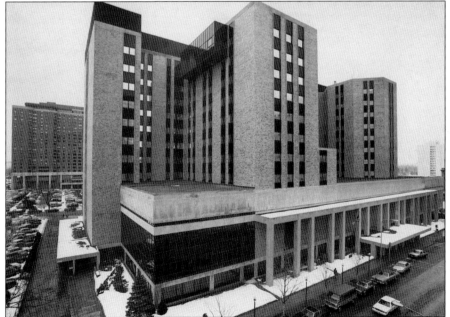

Methodist Hospital, March 3, 1986. *Courtesy Rochester Post-Bulletin*

FLOOD & REDEVELOPMENT 1978-1999

Soldiers Field Swimming Pool, August 1987. *Courtesy Rochester Post-Bulletin*

Chicago Great Western "Save the Depot" fund drive during Rochesterfest, 1987.
Courtesy Olmsted County Historical Society

Seibens Building being built where the 1914 Mayo Clinic building once stood, September 1987. *Courtesy Olmsted County Historical Society*

Marion Baihly speaking to visitors at the Fall Flower Festival at Mayowood, September 13, 1987. *Courtesy Olmsted County Historical Society*

The Olmsted County Courthouse, 1989. *Courtesy Rochester Post-Bulletin*

Construction underway in downtown Rochester as part of a project which transformed Rochester's skyline with $80 million of new construction, December 27, 1988. The project included the Radisson Centerplace Hotel, Galleria shopping mall, parking ramps, and the Mayo Clinic's Seibens building. *Courtesy Rochester Post-Bulletin*

FLOOD & REDEVELOPMENT 1978-1999

Mayor Chuck Hazama at the "tree raising" at the Kahler Plaza Hotel, 1988. City Council President Nancy Selby is on the left. *Courtesy Olmsted County Historical Society*

Entrance to Rochester's IBM facilities, 1990. IBM came to Rochester in the 1950s and became one of Rochester's principal industries. *Courtesy Rochester Post-Bulletin*

An aerial view of Rochester, May 1990. *Courtesy Rochester Post-Bulletin*

The recently completed Siebens Building at the Mayo Clinic, October 24, 1989. *Courtesy Rochester Post-Bulletin*

Downtown Rochester skyway on 2nd Street S.W., September 1990. *Courtesy Rochester Post-Bulletin*

An aerial view of Rochester Community College, February 1990. *Courtesy Rochester Post-Bulletin*

FLOOD & REDEVELOPMENT 1978-1999

Federal Medical Center, August 8, 1990. The federal prison opened in 1985, using facilities of the former Rochester State Hospital which closed in 1981. The facility has housed such high-profile figures such as former television evangelist Jim Baker. *Courtesy Rochester Post-Bulletin*

The Rochester Mustangs junior hockey team, September 27, 1991. Head coach Mark Kaufman talks with the team before they take the ice at a game at the Rochester-Olmsted Recreation Center. The Mustangs won the national championship in 1989. *Courtesy Rochester Post-Bulletin*

The new Mayo Civic Center, March 30, 1991. Located in historic Mayo Park, the original Mayo Civic Auditorium opened in 1939. The statues of the Mayo brothers located in front of the building were dedicated in 1952. *Courtesy Rochester Post-Bulletin*

CELEBRATING 150 YEARS

Bumper boat ride at the Olmsted County Fair, August 1993. *Courtesy Rochester Post-Bulletin*

Mai Xo Yang, left, Chong Chang, middle, and Yer Chang display Hmong outfits to students at Holmes Elementary School, March 25, 1992. *Courtesy Rochester Post-Bulletin*

A giant balloon in the 1990 Rochesterfest parade. The first Rochesterfest was held in 1983 as one of the festivities to celebrate Rochester's 125th anniversary. *Courtesy Rochester Post-Bulletin*

Warren Lucio, 7, does a traditional ceremonial dance at the intertribal powwow in Rochester, April 23, 1998. *Courtesy Rochester Post-Bulletin*

Justices of the Minnesota Supreme Court came to Rochester on February 3, 1995. Left to right: Paul Anderson, Sandra Gardebring, M. Jeanne Coyne, Chief Justice A.M. "Sandy" Keith, Esther Tomljanovich, Alan Page and Edward Stringer. Justice Keith is a Rochester native. *Courtesy Rochester Post-Bulletin*

The Rochester Skeeters during their 1998 home opener against Billings at the Mayo Civic Auditorium. The Skeeters played two seasons in Rochester. *Courtesy Rochester Post-Bulletin*

Joggers along a bicycle and walking path east of the Silver Lake Power Plant on the Zumbro River, 1998. The paths were created during a massive flood control project that transformed the city while protecting it from future floods. *Courtesy Rochester Post-Bulletin*

A New Millennium 2000 - Today

As someone said of the weather: "If you want to know what the weather will be tomorrow, look outside." That holds true for history. Rochester's economy today is affected by national and global trends. As in the past, the medical industry has remained strong. Despite the terrorist attacks on the World Trade Center of 9/11, combined with a global economic downturn, Rochester's main industry is less affected than other economic areas.

Today, towering cranes punctuate the sky as construction downtown continues. Mayo Clinic has announced future plans for a new medical campus and the city's population continues to grow. University Center Rochester is a robust higher education force in southeastern Minnesota and the city is examining ways to upgrade K-12 educational opportunities in the community.

The Rochester air traffic continues to be healthy for passengers and air cargo helped by its status as an International Airport with its own customs officer. Air freight promises a potential for growth as Minneapolis-St. Paul International is reaching cargo capacity.

The recently expanded Mayo Civic Center has capacity for larger conventions that will add to the market for lodging and food service in the city. New multi-screen movie complexes offer an expanded film experience here. Amateur sports offerings continue to grow.

And, opportunities for recreation in city and county parks and programs continue to flourish and grow in promise for the future. 150 years ago, George Head probably could not foresee what his town would be today. We suffer a similar myopia. However, if history is any harbinger, Rochester is destined to offer residents an unmatched quality of life for another 150 years.

An aerial view of downtown Rochester, August 14, 2001, showing major redevelopment that took place in the 1990s. The government center is in the right foreground. *Courtesy Rochester Post-Bulletin*

Dedication of Veterans Memorial at Soldiers Field Memorial Park, June 2000. The memorial's granite walls have engraved war scenes and the names of Rochester area men and women who died in battle or from battle injuries. *Courtesy Rochester Post-Bulletin*

CELEBRATING 150 YEARS

Front page of the Rochester Post-Bulletin, September 11, 2001. *Courtesy Rochester Post-Bulletin*

Mourners add to the memorial in front of the massive bronze doors of the Plummer Building closed following the attacks of September 11, 2001, on the World Trade Center in New York and the Pentagon in Washington, D.C. *Courtesy Rochester Post-Bulletin*

Andy Mulholland, 17, stands on the 55th Street bridge paying tribute to those who died in the terrorist attacks, September 12, 2001. *Courtesy Rochester Post-Bulletin*

Mohamed Abdullahi Rage, 68, waved an American flag during a rally held by the Rochester Islamic Center to denounce terrorism. *Courtesy Rochester Post-Bulletin*

A NEW MILLENNIUM 2000-TODAY

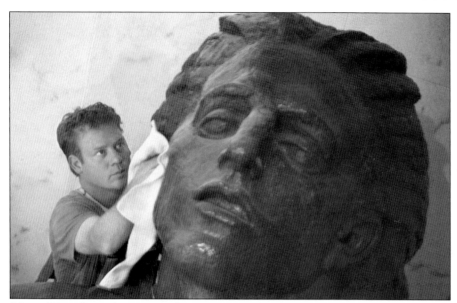

Man of Freedom, the massive bronze statue that had been on the Mayo Building exterior since 1952, was moved to the new Gonda Building, September 2001. *Courtesy Rochester Post-Bulletin*

The 20-story Gonda Building became the newest of the Mayo Clinic facilities, October 2001. At a cost of $375 million, it was Rochester's largest-ever building project. *Courtesy Rochester Post-Bulletin*

Man of Freedom hangs on the wall of the new Gonda Building atrium. The building opened on October 8, 2001, after three years of construction. *Courtesy Rochester Post-Bulletin*

CELEBRATING 150 YEARS

Rochester's volleyball team, the Minnesota Chill, celebrate becoming United States Professional Volleyball Champions, May 6, 2001. *Courtesy Rochester Post-Bulletin*

Youth gathered at the Rochester skatepark, located at west Silver Lake, September 6, 2002. *Courtesy Rochester Post-Bulletin*

Swimmers enjoy a summer day at Foster Arend beach, August 2, 2002. *Courtesy Rochester Post-Bulletin*

Michael Restovich, left, had just been called up by the Minnesota Twins, September 17, 2002. He was a 1997 Rochester Mayo High School graduate. *Courtesy Rochester Post-Bulletin*

A NEW MILLENNIUM 2000-TODAY

A hot air balloon readies for an ascent during Rochesterfest, June 13, 2002. *Courtesy Rochester Post-Bulletin*

Protestors at South Broadway and 2nd Street N.W. expressed their views on the war with Iraq, March 18, 2003. Andrew Moe, left, was against the war while the other students, right, supported the war effort. *Courtesy Rochester Post-Bulletin*

Construction of the UCR Regional Sports Center, May 2002. *Courtesy Rochester Post-Bulletin*

David Sletten and Kathe Ruebel watched at Buffalo Wild Wings in northwest Rochester on March 20, 2003, as President George W. Bush made a statement from the Oval Office that the war with Iraq had begun. *Courtesy Rochester Post-Bulletin*